How to Be a **SUPERSTAR** Salesperson

AUDRI WHITE

First Edition

Fulton Books, Inc.
Meadville, PA

Published by Fulton Books 2021

ISBN 978-1-64952-970-1 (paperback)
ISBN 978-1-64952-971-8 (digital)

Printed in the United States of America

CONTENTS

INTRODUCTION

Have you ever wondered what it takes to be a superstar salesperson? This individual is highly effective in his sales position (he/she knows the business, they win many accolades and rewards, and it's a well-known fact that they make more money than most of their coworkers). They are highly valued by both his company and his customers. Let's call him or her the sales professional, *Sales Pro* for short.

Sales Pros are highly successful year after year in their respective industries. You might have also noticed that there is no one type. They may be older or younger, tall or short, male or female, conservative or progressive. You simply cannot tell by looking at them, but trust me, they all have something very much in common. They have learned what all Sales Pros already know. They are keenly aware that there are five key areas where technique and know-how are imperative if you hope to be highly successful in the world of sales.

These five areas are:

1. the ability to make a connection,
2. getting in front of potential prospects,
3. knowing how to have a highly effective initial sales call,
4. handling objections or resolving questions or concerns, and
5. closing and walking away with your goal.

This book is for you if you are just getting started and appreciate the importance of establishing a strong foundation. However, it is also for you if you are looking for a system that will help you upgrade your current skills, leading to greater success.

CHAPTER 1

The Art of Connecting

The Art of Connecting

In order to sell anything to anybody, you must first make a connection.

The CAPI System

CAPI is a sales technique that helps you to "break the ice" when meeting someone for the first time. Each letter stands for a practice that you must do in this exact order for full effectiveness.

C stands for *Connecting* or having an exchange where two people acknowledge each other.

A stands for *Affirming* where something positive is shared by the Sales Pro.

P stands for *Permission*, and this happens when the Sales Pro asks if the prospect would mind them sharing some information, typically part of their sales story or their pitch.

I stands for *Inform* which is where the Sales Pro shares what he has to offer and how it can be beneficial to the prospect. The goal here is to set an appointment date and time.

Let's look at how CAPI works by using an example.

CAPI Example One

We'll assume that Karen Winters is our Sales Pro. She is the manager at the local toy store, Imagine. She has been building her business with fliers in the local newspaper and by word of mouth. She happens to be in the grocery store checkout line behind a friendly mom and her two little girls. Let's watch the CAPI system work starting with step one.

Connecting: Think about how easily we connect with family and friends. These are people with whom we already have a relationship; however, most people you will be selling to are perfect strangers.

Learning how to connect will give you infinitely more sales opportunities. Karen will first want to make eye contact. She is not staring but acknowledging presence. She might add a greeting like "how are you?" or maybe "isn't this the most gorgeous day?" Now, if you get a grunt or no response at all, no worries. You haven't lost anything. Each person you talk to will have a totally different unpredictable response. It's quite all right to simply say, "Have a nice day," as you're thinking to yourself, *So what*, and, *On to the next one*. Remember, it's a numbers game, so we cannot allow someone's sullen attitude to shut us down.

Affirming: Karen needs to say something positive, so how about something thoughtful about the girls like "are they always so polite?" Most moms would be pleased to hear a nice compliment about their children's behavior. This takes us to our next action.

Permission: Here is where you ask your prospect if it's okay to share something with them. It's important to actually get their permission because once it's given, they are obliged to listen to you. The final step is *I*.

Informing: In this case, Karen says, "My name is Karen Winters, and I manage Imagine, the toy store over on Main. I just wondered if you are familiar with us. We carry the country's most popular toys and games for school-aged children like your beautiful daughters, and I'd like to invite you to come visit the store. We're having a great sale right now. Children and parents love our selections because we always carry the skill-building games that are designed to improve memory, math, and reading." Note that Karen already knows what to say about her store and what the benefits are of shopping there (pitch). She also invites the family to come there by a certain time. She has done a great job of giving the mom a reason to visit her store.

CAPI Example Two

Let's look at a second CAPI example. Our Sales Pro Fred has just arrived at the home of a good friend, Bill. Bill is hosting his annual fourth of July cookout. One other guest has already arrived,

Charles, who is in the backyard with his two sons. Fred makes his way to the backyard and introduces himself to Charles as he takes a seat at the picnic table.

FRED. Happy fourth, I'm Fred. Nice to meet you. It's Charles, right? Bill mentioned that you two worked together at Apex.

CHARLES. Good to meet you too. Bill and I go back a few years now since I started at the company, and those two over there with the baseball are my two sons, Kevin and Mark.

Connecting

FRED. Good-looking sons you have, athletic too! How old are they?

CHARLES. Well, Kevin, the oldest, is seven, and Mark is five next month. How about you, any kids yet?

FRED. I have a four-year-old daughter. She lives with her mom. They couldn't make it today.

CHARLES. My wife, Anne, would love to try again for a little girl, but I really don't know with the way the costs of everything is skyrocketing.

FRED. Yeah, I know. I've spent a lot of time lately thinking about how to get ready for my daughter's college education. I know that with the cost of tuition, if I don't have something in place, it's going to be nearly impossible for her to go. Have you thought about it with two boys so close in age?

CHARLES. Oh, yes, it's what keeps me up at night.

Affirming

FRED. Your boys sure know how to handle a baseball. Maybe they'll play sports and win some athletic scholarship money, why not?

CHARLES. They do love baseball. That's just something we cannot rely on.

Permission

FRED. Charles, do you mind if I ask you a question. (*Fred waits for permission.*)

CHARLES. Sure, just don't ask for any money. (*He laughs.*)

Inform

FRED. No, I promise, but I would like to ask you for some of your time. You see, I'm an advisor for Ball State Insurance Company, and I would appreciate the opportunity to sit down with you and your spouse to show you a couple of different ways of planning for your family and, in particular, the education of your two boys. This is information you need to know about based on your concerns. After all, who's going to be there for the kids if we aren't. How about we get together next week?

CHARLES. Okay, how about Tuesday after work. Right now, Let's grab some of those hot dogs!

In the examples, our Sales Pros made appointments using CAPI. This may take five minutes, or it might fifteen minutes. Do exercise patience and remember to do each step in order. Be sure to wait for permission for the best effectiveness.

Building Rapport

According to Google, "rapport is a connection or relationship with someone else." It can be considered as a state of harmonious understanding with another individual or group. Building rapport is the process of developing that connection with someone else.

Whether you are in your company's conference room or your friend's backyard for a cookout, building rapport with a potential client is crucial because it does two things: it lets your prospect know that you see them as more than just a potential sale, and they have the opportunity to know you as more than simply someone who wants a sale from them. Successful rapport building should allow for an exchange of knowledge both personal and business which eventually leads to an increased level of trust. This trust factor is often what makes an individual or company the vendor of choice.

It is not necessary to be friends with your prospects in order to do business. You may have seen some in sales giving away gifts and tickets to special events in order to win favor, but the truth is there's simply no substitute for meeting your customer's needs at a price they can afford. You are a professional, much like a doctor or lawyer. You are in their life to provide a product or service for which you have much knowledge, so while you may become good friends over time, it is important to be the sales professional offering the best possible advice. Trust is earned by you being good at what you do and delivering on what you promise.

Rapport building is easy when two people have something in common. Let's assume you're in someone's home or office. If you check the walls, you may see diplomas or certificates, artwork, or photography. On the desk, there may be pictures of family or friends. There may be a trophy case or collectibles of some kind which is a clue about your prospect's hobbies or interests. Use these items as an opportunity to start your rapport building. Most people enjoy talking about their family and friends or an enjoyable pastime like sports or collecting. Make a note about their interests so that you can ask questions about their involvement and get to know them better. Let's say Mike, our copier Sales Pro, is in Mr. Smith's office after getting the first appointment, and he notices a set of golf clubs in the corner. This is their first meeting, and they don't know each other at all, but that bag of golf clubs can be an ice breaker because Mike is also learning to play, so the questions come easy. They might sound like this: "Mr. Smith, I see your clubs over there, how long have you played?" or "where do you like to play around here?" or "any advice for someone who is just getting started?" Please note that the best questions are open-ended. You want more than a yes or no answer. Also, make sure it's your prospect doing most of the talking. It's your time to listen and get to know him or her. Make notes so that you can build on this topic and listen for other interests that they might share. This is where listening skills are so important. We'll talk about listening shortly.

Don't be alarmed if it seems that you have nothing in common because *everyone has something in common*! Everyone loves their family, and everyone loves their friends, and most people have an interest outside of work. They usually enjoy talking about them even to complete strangers at times. Everyone has something that they like and don't like about their jobs, and everyone usually has a take on what is peculiar about their hometowns—be it the weather or the baseball team. Don't neglect to bone up on what's happening in sports or business or the local celebrity in your backyard. These are topics you will want to know because they make a great ice breaker.

If you are a bit uncomfortable right now because you're new at this, don't worry. I was too at the start of my sales career. It made me more uncomfortable than any other part of the sales cycle. But now, I enjoy building rapport more than anything. Practice patiently, you will be doing it naturally before you know it.

CHAPTER 2

Getting in Front of Your Prospects

Getting in Front of Your Prospects

For many in professional sales, an appointment is required, and we are not familiar with our prospect. The appointment may be made by phone, online, or in person, but a good pitch is always required to make it happen. There are four (4) requirements for the pitch. The pitch must be *short and sweet, have a purpose and be able to capture attention by providing a value, and finally asking for the meeting*.

The best way to show this is with a couple of examples. In our first example, Mike the copier Sales Pro is attempting to meet the controller who signs off on all new copier sales for Apex International. "Good morning, Mr. Smith, I hope your day is going well"—waits for the answer—"my name is Mike White, your copier specialist for this area, and I would really appreciate spending a few minutes with you to introduce myself to you in case you run into any immediate or future needs regarding your copy equipment. I'd like to show you how we can help your documents look their best while increasing productivity. Would you have a few minutes tomorrow morning around 10:00 a.m.?"

Let's take a look at the call. First, it is short and sweet. Secondly, there is a purpose; to make an introduction. Thirdly, there is a value for the business; how to put their best foot forward while increasing productivity. Lastly, Mike did ask for the appointment.

Let's look at a second example: Fred, our advisor from Ball State Insurance, is seeking a meeting with Ms. O'Conner to discuss her financial plan. "Hello, Ms. O'Conner. Thank you for your time this evening. I'll just be a few minutes. My name is Fred Price from Ball State Insurance in downtown Milwaukee, and I'm calling to talk with you about your financial plan to be sure it is still providing adequate protection for you and your family. You have had it for a few years, and we need to see if it is still adequate for you. It might require one or two adjustments, and it is possible that we may even be able to save you some money. Can we meet this week, say Thursday evening?"

In looking at this example, we have a call that is short and sweet, the purpose is to check for plan adequacy since it has been a few years. It may require an adjustment or two, and there is value in confirming this, and also there is a possibility of saving some costs, and finally a meeting time is requested. I'm sure that you already know that you won't get an appointment with every call. Making appointments is a numbers game too. The more calls you make, the more appointments you'll get and the better you become at making these appointments. I cannot overstate the importance of actually practicing. The confidence that you gain will make all the difference in your success.

The Effective Sales Call: the Key to Your Success

Now that you have successfully made your appointment, you want to be sure to make the most of it. We are assuming this is the first call. If it's not successful, you probably won't have a second chance. We need to get this right. The idea is to get to know as much as you can about your prospect and their company while assuring them that there is a good reason for them to spend time with you. Sometimes in the first meeting, the prospect will attempt to rush you by asking you to just show them what you have so that they can very quickly decide whether to give you their time or move on. It is important that your prospect understand that you have a number of different products or services that could be recommended, but it would be unfair to them if you were not to take the time to understand some key points about their operation. An effective sales call should have an opening pitch which should convince the prospect that you have something worth hearing about. Your opening line should pique the interest with something valuable and ask for their attention. We gain our understanding through a series of questions. If they cannot give you this time, it's better to reschedule the meeting rather than rush through since this will only shortchange both you and them. An example of an opening statement or pitch for Mike, our copier salesman, might sound like this, "Mr. Smith, I have been able to reduce costs by ten to twenty-five percent in the companies that I work for, and I'd like to do the same for you if you're interested. Will you give me a few minutes this morning?"

An opening statement for Fred, the financial advisor, might sound like this, "Charles, I'd like to create a plan for you that would protect your family and grow your assets at the same time. Would you give me some time to show you how this can work for you?"

Both opening statements provide a value to the prospect and request their time and attention.

CHAPTER 3

SPIN and FAB

SPIN and FAB

Let's take a look at where an effective sales call originates. It begins with a questioning technique called SPIN. This is followed by a pre-close technique which we identify as FAB. Below is the meaning of each:

- *S* (situation questions)
- *P* (problem questions)
- *I* (implication questions)
- *N* (needs-payoff questions)

plus

- *F* (features)
- *A* (advantage)
- *B* (benefits)

Situation questions: These are the questions that give you a general overview of the operation. These are the who, what, where, when and how questions that inform you of how well your competition is working. For our copier salesman, a few standard questions should include: What type of equipment is currently being used? What do the primary copy jobs look like? What do the larger jobs involve? Do they have any special requirements from the equipment? How's your equipment working out for you? How are the purchase decisions made?

Problem questions: your next mission is to find out if they are happy with how things are operating. The problem questions are used to determine this. Your first questions might be: Are their needs being met with the current equipment? What kinds of issues are you seeing with the current product? You might ask, "If you were to make changes, what would they look like?"

Implication questions: here is where we ask our prospect how they and their business has been impacted. We are asking how he or she really feels about the current products and how important it is to make changes. We want to give our prospects a chance to express their concerns and a willingness to make the change. You might ask, "How does your current equipment affect the productivity in your office?"

Needs-payoff questions: these questions are used to ask your prospect if he or she is willing to purchase from you if you can provide the solution to his current issues and concerns.

SPIN Questions Plus FAB—Example One

We have Mike, our copier Sales Pro from Mainframe 2000, who has arrived for his meeting with Mr. Smith, the controller for Apex International.

They have exchanged pleasantries, and Mike has used his rapport building skills in the first few minutes and is ready to get down to business.

MIKE: Mr. Smith, do you mind if I take some notes. This helps me to stay on track.

MR. SMITH. Not at all, go right ahead.

SPIN Questions

MIKE. Just double-checking, you mentioned that you have four small copiers for each corner of the first floor where sales and admin are located. You also have two mid-sized machines on the second floor to service IT and finance. Generally, what kind of copies are made in each area? (Situation)

MR. SMITH. Well, in sales and admin, you'll see mostly onesies and two-sies. In finance and IT, they tend to have a higher volume. IT is responsible for the training manuals, and the records kept by Finance tend to be multiple original for one copy set. Scanning the document to save, and e-mail has cut down on paper use significantly.

MIKE. Sounds like you have several different applications requiring different features on both floors.

MR. SMITH. Yes, this is correct. The two Yamaha 3000s in finance and IT are better suited to handle more originals, and they are fast with the ability to collate and staple.

MIKE. Mr. Smith, who decides which copiers are the best for your office? (Situation)

MR. SMITH. I make most purchase decisions, and I usually have my assistant review everything, you know, a second set of eyes.

MIKE. Mr. Smith, you also mentioned there is a need to visit other departments to use different machines. Does this cause any issues? (Problem)

MR. SMITH. As a matter of fact, we know that there is a slowdown in productivity just from the time that it takes to move between the different areas and also because of the socializing or water cooler effect that happens when two or more people are waiting in line. When the smaller copiers are down, the midsize copiers come into play, and finance and IT don't like sharing because now they have to wait to use their own machines and their productivity is affected. This also creates more waste since all of the employees are not as familiar with how these copiers work.

MIKE. So how often does this happen and how exactly does it impact productivity? (Implication)

MR. SMITH. It happens constantly. The backup is real as some of the employees wind up staying late to get work finished. This impacts the payroll as well as productivity which can be hard to put a finger on.

MIKE. These are important concerns. How does this affect you personally? (Implication)

MR. SMITH. Well, I've certainly heard enough complaints, and I understand that nobody likes staying late to get their work done. I know that our profitability is affected, and I need to fix it.

MIKE. It sounds like the machines in this current environment are underperforming, not offering all of the needed features. Please correct me if I'm wrong, but it sounds like you are saying that all of this affects your costs and productivity. If I could show you a configuration that would provide the features that you really need on both floors, speed and versatility, and show you different ways to lower your costs, would you be interested in making a change? (Needs-payoff question)

MR. SMITH. Yes, I would, Mike. I need to make some improvements.

And Now for FAB

MIKE. I know that I have the equipment that will make your operation run a lot smoother. The copiers that I have in mind for the first and second floors will be twice as fast as your current models. At forty (40) copies per minute, copy jobs will get finished a lot faster (FEATURE). This will also cut down on the time spent waiting in line and reduce the water cooler effect that is affecting your productivity (ADVANTAGE). We will also add the features including collating, stapling, and two-sided copying. The duplex or two-sided copying will also reduce the cost of paper typically by twenty percent to forty percent (FEATURE AND ADVANTAGE). This will eliminate the need to leave the first floor to find these features creating a slowdown in the workload and eliminate much if not all of the overtime required to complete work (ADVANTAGE). This will increase productivity and lower payroll expense which leads to increased profits. I also believe your employees will be generally happier to have the equipment that makes their jobs easier (BENEFIT).

MR. SMITH. Sounds great! I'm looking forward to seeing your suggestions in writing!

When Mike returns on Friday, he should summarize what he learned in the previous meeting before making his recommendations. He should then repeat the FAB method in his proposal which explains why his proposal makes perfect sense for his prospect.

Benefits drive us to make purchase decisions, so it is highly useful to use FAB in all proposals. Be sure to drive home your benefits provided by the new plan.

SPIN Questions Plus FAB Example Two

Our financial adviser, Fred, is on a life insurance call with his prospect, Charles.

FRED. Charles, I want to thank you for coming to my office this afternoon. Tell me, what were you thinking about on the way over here? (Situation question)

CHARLES. Well, I was thinking that I hope I can qualify for the insurance that I want and that I can afford to pay for it.

FRED. I can understand that and let me assure you that we have several options and can be creative in figuring out how to make it happen. Let me also ask you, if you had a blank canvas and were painting a picture of your financial vision, what would it look like? (Situation question)

CHARLES. My vision is simple. I would just like to take care of my family in the way that they deserve. This would include a nice home, nice cars, and a regular vacation with enough money in the bank to not have to worry so much.

FRED. Tell me more.

CHARLES. Well, we're managing, but I worry about not having a sizable savings in case of an emergency. I also worry about having enough money to educate my two sons.

FRED. Do you ever wonder how your family would manage if you weren't here, and they had to manage without your income? (Problem question)

CHARLES. I do, and that's one of the reasons I'm here. They would not be able to maintain the house, cars, and hopes for college would probably disappear altogether.

FRED. How do you feel about this? (Implication question)

CHARLES. I feel like I want to do something about it as soon as possible. I'm just not sure what to do exactly.

FRED. If I understand you correctly, it sounds like you want to help your family maintain its current lifestyle and put an investment in place to grow in value so that when your sons reach college age, they will have some assistance.

CHARLES. That's right, Fred. What can you do for me?

FRED. We can definitely put some protection in place which can protect the family financially. We can also look at the college savings plans for your young men, or we can consider life insurance plans that grow in value that can provide cash for them to borrow against and still have the life insurance in place.

CHARLES. Sounds good so far, but how much will all this cost?

FRED. Before we price it out, tell me if I can show you the plan that will protect your family's current lifestyle and put away a substantial amount for the boys' education later on, would you be ready to move forward? (Needs-payoff question)

CHARLES. Yes, I absolutely would be willing to put something in place.

And Now for FAB

FRED. I do have some plans for you that include a whole life insurance policy. What this will do is provide from day one the protection that you seek for your family home, cars, and other debt. This will eliminate your concern for your family's comfort if you weren't here. We will also look at whole life insurance plans for the boys that will increase in value with their ages. They will act as college savings plans and life insurance protection so that when they are of college age, there will be some money waiting for them to use. They can count on these policies for life which will have a low cost that will never increase, and naturally, they can always buy more insurance later on. Let me get this all printed up and priced for you. I can come by Saturday morning with the pricing. Is this a good time?

CHARLES. I'm really looking forward to seeing what you have for us. Can you come by at say 11:00 a.m.?

FRED. Great, I'll see you then.

In the previous two examples, we used the SPIN technique to get to the bottom of our prospect's real needs and how they really feel about them. We then tested their willingness to make a change with the Needs-Payoff Question. Once we learned that they were indeed ready to make changes to their current situation, we used FAB (FEATURES, ADVANTAGES, AND BENEFITS) to introduce our product plans. FAB is critical in helping you make your case. We buy because there is a BENEFIT to owning a particular product. Without real BENEFIT, there is no real motivation to buy.

If you're currently selling, you're likely to already have opening statements or pitches and some situation questions that you like to use. You'll want to just be sure that they are designed to give you a very good general understanding of the current operation. Be sure to add problem and implication questions and finally your Needs-Payoff Question and FAB. Your prospect should always be doing most of the talking. How else can you find out what really concerns them? Now is the time to listen very carefully and always verify with your prospect that you understand what they are telling you. For instance, in example one (1), at the Needs-Payoff Question, our Sales Pro says, "Please correct me if I'm wrong, but it sounds like you are saying..."

In example two, our Sales Pro asks his prospect to "tell me more" which encourages the conversation and provides useful information for our Sales Pro to use. He also makes the comment, "If I understand you correctly, it sounds like..." this provides an opportunity to seek clarity.

The Sales Pro must be sure that he understands his prospect prior to making a proposal of any kind or risk losing all credibility.

CHAPTER 4

Objection Handling

Objection Handling

There are an infinite number of objections, so you will surely hear many more than the ones we have listed below. The objections listed below are some of the most common objections you will hear. Please note that although the words may vary slightly from the ones used here; the objection may still fit into one of these four categories.

Objection one: We're just fine. We don't need anything right now.
Sounds like: We'll call you if we need anything.
Objection two: We're too busy right now.
Sounds like: Call us back in a few months.
Objection three: Already we're using ABC brand.
Sounds like: We're happy with our current supplier.
Objection four: We don't have the money.
Sounds like: We can't afford it right now, or (for some companies) we're waiting for approval in the new budget.

Objections Example One

Objection one: We're just fine. Let's assume that Fred, our financial advisor, is making appointments for next week and runs into objection number one.

FRED. Ms. O'Conner, I'm glad that you feel everything is okay, but please know that your financial plan tends to require updating at least once a year because for the average person, important life changes happen approximately every six months. How long has it been since your last review? Think about it, what important changes have you experienced? For example, a change in jobs in the family, marriage, divorce, a new baby, or grandchild. Maybe you've bought or sold a home, experienced a death in the family, or maybe a child getting ready for college. Any one of these events signal the need for a plan review. It's critical to be sure that the plan is still serving you in the way that you need it to. Your plan is fluid and needs to be managed. I hope that you can understand this, Ms. O'Conner. I can meet with you this Friday. Does this work for you?

Note: Many people will tell you they are fine when they really are not. It's important to have these review opportunities. Guess who they will hold responsible if they come to realize that changes should have been made that didn't happen?

Objection two: I'm too busy right now. "Mr. Harper, I understand that you're busy right now, but your financial plan is just about as important as your health, and I'm sure that you would not ignore your health or the health of a family member because you are busy. It's important to take care of your plan so that when you need it, it's ready to take care of you. It is time for your review, so let's get together. I'm open Tuesday or Thursday of this week. Which day works best for you?

Note: Fred did a great job of creating urgency here so that his customer understands the importance of their meeting.

Objection three: We use ABC brand. "Ms. Mendes, I can appreciate that everything seems just fine right now, but it always seems that way until you need something. How long ago was your last review? Do you know if your price is competitive? I do all of this for you at no charge. And it only takes a small amount of time. Wouldn't you agree that it's time well spent? What day this week is best for you?"

Objection four: We don't have the money. "Mr. Jones, if you don't have the money for your financial plan right now, you probably won't have the money next month or next year. The purpose of our meeting is to make sure that you and your family are protected and provided a savings vehicle so that over time, you will have a fund that you can use when you need it. It sounds like we should get together to go over your options. Would Monday night work for you?"

Objections Example Two

Now, let's look at Mike, our copier Sales Pro as he handles these same objections from his business customers.

Objection one: we're just fine. "Mr. Smith, I'm glad to know that everything is okay for now, but they are machines that get used constantly by different people all day long. It's only a matter of time. They will break down and they will need attention. I'd like you to have my information so that you can call me, and I can respond quickly to any need that may come about. I'm in your area tomorrow. Is morning or afternoon better?"

Objection two: I'm too busy right now. "I appreciate your schedule, Mr. Smith. This is why I'd like to meet with you as soon as possible. I know the role that copiers can play in downtime, wasted supplies, and reduced productivity. The right equipment means increased productivity and less downtime and waste. This also means less headaches for you. Wouldn't you agree with me that it wouldn't hurt to spend a few minutes? I'm in your area on Tuesday. How about lunch?"

Objection three: we'll keep what we have. Sounds like: "We already have a copier company."

"It sounds like you give most of your business to one company. I know that this might seem convenient, but are you sure this is in your best interest when it comes to price, service, and the latest technology? I've known a few companies who have felt this way only to learn that they paid a price for not looking into the newer, more efficient models. Quality and productivity can be drastically different with copiers as I'm sure you know. I promise not to take up too much of your time. Can we meet Friday afternoon?"

Objection four: we don't have the money. Sounds like: "We don't have the money to make changes right now."

"Mr. Smith, I have to tell you that I believe this is all the more reason we should meet. I've been able to get many of my customers into brand-new equipment that is less expensive to operate, less wasteful, and actually increases productivity. I should also mention that our payment options often make buying new equipment the better decision. Can you spare a few minutes tomorrow afternoon? I'd love to show you how we could work for you."

Note: Show understanding for their position, create urgency, and always ask for the appointment. Also, be C*onfident.* Prospects find it easy to believe if they know that you believe.

CHAPTER 5

What "No" Really Means

What "No" Really Means

Anyone who has ever sold anything (even the very best Sales Pros) has heard the word *NO*. You can be at the very top of your game, and you will still hear it because no one in the world closes at one hundred percent. It's important to understand how you feel when you hear the word *NO*, especially when you've worked really hard and totally expected to win the business. *Too often, we personalize the NO making us feel rejected.* It tends to have a similar effect on everyone, even the toughest among us.

We talk about it because it is real, and it impacts all of us. We don't want it to affect us anymore than it should. No matter how badly you might feel about not getting the sale, do keep in mind that it rarely has anything to do with you personally. It's important to recognize these feelings so that you can shake them off as soon as you can. These feelings are dangerous because they can cost you money if you allow yourself to be negatively affected.

We need to know what makes us feel better. Whether it's hanging out with friends, a new pair of shoes, or a nice long run in the park, let's do it and get on with our life. If we take a closer look at the "no," we can see it as our partner along the journey to the "Yes." Think about it, most prospects are not going to say yes. You could be providing the best, the smartest, and the most wonderful product, yet most prospects are not going to buy from you. The good news is you don't need everyone to buy from you. *Your real job is to get through the No types so that you can get to your Yes types. Remember, sales is a numbers game.* Know your own personal numbers. On the average, how many "Noes" do you need to get to your "Yes" customers. In other words, what is your **close ratio**? How many prospects do you need to see in order to get a closing? If your goal is five sales per month, and you close every 3 prospects, then you will need to meet and sell fifteen prospects each month.

Another very important fact to keep in mind, the *no* types give a chance to practice your presentation lines, your objection handling, and your closing skills. Use the *no* types to sharpen your skills. After each call, take a few minutes and think about what you learned.

Consider how you would do it differently next time. If it wasn't for this practice, we could never become Sales Pros.

So the next time you hear the word *no,* simply smile and say, "Thank you for your time. Let's stay in touch," and, "NEXT!"

CHAPTER 6

The Art of Listening

The Art of Listening

We've talked a lot about what kind of questions to ask and how to respond in sales situations. A lot of salespeople believe that it is their job to do most of the talking even more than their prospects. There is a time to talk, like when you are explaining your proposal or solution to improve their situation. Your primary job is to find out what your prospects want and need, and then to find the solution. This can only be achieved by asking the right questions and listening carefully to the answers.

Focused Listening

Have you ever noticed how two intelligent people can listen to the same narrative and come away with two totally different takes on what was just heard? The reality is that no two people listen the same way. Our listening skills are affected by how well we hear, how focused we are, and our own personal filters of our past experiences. These factors cause us to hear conversations, even view situations very differently than someone else might.

Practice active listening in order to hear better. Recall from the examples in the SPIN chapter, our Sales Pro practiced active listening techniques. In one case, our copier Sales Pro Mike said, "If I am hearing you correctly," he also asked to take notes so that he could follow along better. Fred, our advisor, also used the line "tell me more." This type of language both encourages your prospect to talk more and helps you to hear more and confirm that you have heard correctly. Imagine going away from your sales call with the wrong idea or not being totally clear about your prospect's needs. Your proposal will be off base, and the big opportunity to win them over is instead a huge fail.

Never underestimate the importance of listening. You'll probably only have one chance to get their story right.

Tips for Effective Listening

Here are some tips for effective listening. Though you probably already know these suggestions, they are so important that I would like to take the time to reiterate them.

Tip one. Block out all distractions if you can. If you have chosen to meet in a place that is too noisy to hear well, make a change if you can. This also shows how important the meeting is to your client.

Tip two. Do nothing else during your meeting time. Planning your call like what you want to share with your prospect about you and your company, questions you plan to ask, and what other information you need to collect should be done in advance of the meeting. Anticipate the objections before the meeting so you are prepared to handle them, and you can concentrate on listening.

Tip three. I know it's hard but turn off the phone. I've watched a ringing cell phone completely ruin a well-planned sales call. It causes a loss of focus and sometimes a loss of interest. Should you risk this?

Tip four. Ask if it's okay to take notes. Most customers don't mind at all. Some will be impressed by your organization. It will help you keep track of the important facts being shared and often leads you to asking better questions.

Tip five. Don't hesitate to ask your prospect to repeat something because you want to be sure you understand completely. It demonstrates your concern about getting it right, and it helps you to make the right recommendations.

CHAPTER 7

Close to Win

Close to Win

The final step in your sales presentation is the CLOSE. This is the moment when you present your proposal or solution. Your goal is to turn your prospect into your new customer. We do this by closing or asking for the business.

Closing is fully expected by your prospect. You wouldn't have a sales meeting in the first place if you weren't planning to make your prospect a new customer. It is the natural conclusion and final step in any sales cycle

Discomfort with Closing

Closing is viewed by many in sales as the most uncomfortable part of the sales cycle. Some feel awkward about asking for something, others see it as aggressive somehow, and some are afraid of the "No," so they hesitate to ask for the business.

The reality is your prospect is fully expecting you to ask for the business once you've done your job and provided them with a solution. They may be wondering why you haven't asked them yet. Additionally, *if you don't ask, someone else will. Then, they will walk away with the business that you have spent precious time and energy trying to win.*

Not asking for the sale is like going to the grocery store and buying a beautiful T-bone steak. You bring it home, turn on the grill, season it well, grill it to perfection, plate it up, sit it on the table in front of you, and just stare at it. You never savor even a tiny piece. In other words, you do all the hard work, but you don't ask for your payoff. *You must ask for the business.*

Closing Techniques

There are several closing techniques. The Needs-Payoff Question in the SPIN technique is a way to pre-close your prospect. You have already asked them if they will do business with you if you can provide a solution to their uncomfortable situation. This is called the upfront closing technique. Another type of closing is to close throughout the presentation. Finally, there is the classic close which is saved for the end of your sales presentation.

Let's look at an example of each.

Upfront or pre-closing. "Mr. and Mrs. O'Conner, I am here today to review the package that I put together for you and your family. If I can show you how Ball State Insurance Company can provide the protection and growth opportunity that you asked for, is there anything that would prevent you from getting started with us today?"

Note: In this case, you are asking for a commitment before sharing the details of the solution. This closing choice is good to use when your prospect is hard to read. It will help you get a better understanding of where you stand with your prospect.

Close throughout the presentation. This method allows you to ask closing questions throughout the call in order to take the temperature of your prospect so to speak and learn what tends to excite them. It also allows the prospect to participate by saying out loud what they like or not. This provides you with more information to tailor your final close.

Closing questions that presume that the prospect is ready to do business.

Example 1:

- "The savings plan portion of the policy can be used for college in another fifteen years. How does this make you feel, Mr. O'Conner?"
- "If Suzie wins a college scholarship, what else might you use the savings for?"

Example 2:

- "Mr. Smith, how do you think your employees will feel about the faster, more versatile equipment?"
- "Mr. Smith, we've provided two different payment plans for the new equipment. Which one suits you better?"
- "In both examples, we are assuming the sale. It's simply a matter of the prospect making some final decisions."

The Classic Close. The third type of closing is the classic close at the end of the presentation.

Example 1A:

- "Mr. Smith, I want to thank you for your time and consideration of our proposal. Now that you have reviewed the price plans, which one shall we write up?"

Example 1B:

- "Mr. Smith, the equipment will take about two weeks to deliver. With a check today, I can get your order in and deliver by the end of the month."

Example 2A:

- "Mr. and Mrs. O'Conner, I'm headed toward my office. I'd be happy to take your check with me. I'll get your application in the system today and your coverage would be in place tomorrow."

Example 2B:

- "Let's get your savings started as soon as possible. A check from you today can get it started tomorrow."

CHAPTER 8

Conclusion

Conclusion

In the social media age that we live in, there's a whole lot of glitz, glam, and hype. It can be a challenge to know the real from the fake, especially when you have so many people pretending a reality often so that they can sell you something, and many others simply trying to satisfy their overly large egos by doing whatever it takes to be "relevant."

What you have here in this "pocket trainer" is a straightforward guide on how to be effective at the science of selling. By the way, *How to be a Super Star Sales Person* is not just for salespeople. Many of us sell regardless of our occupation. Many of us need to sell our ideas, new products, and designs in order to make a successful living. Even parents find themselves selling to their children. I think that we can agree that we all sell.

The real value of this Pocket Trainer is that as you learn this material and become better at selling, you will become better at servicing your prospects, customers, and clients. The benefits of this improved service are increased rewards and greater job satisfaction.

Enjoy the journey to becoming a Super Star Salesperson!

Credits: I was first introduced to the CAPI principle at an Isagenix conference where David Woods was the instructor, and I was trained in the SPIN technique while working in my first sales position at the Xerox Corporation.

ABOUT THE AUTHOR

Audri learned her SPIN technique as a new up-and-coming representative for the Xerox Corporation. She enjoyed a successful career practicing the technique on a daily basis. She began as an account representative, was promoted to major account representative, sales specialist, and trainer/program manager. She credits her rise to the number one sales rep in the country to her training and use of this very special technique. Audri's business background also includes banking and mortgage lending as well as corporate recruiting.

How to Be a Superstar Salesperson is a fusion of Audri's love of writing and her continued love of training. A few years ago, she noticed that her husband's sales team might benefit from having some additional sales tools since many of them, while successful in their own rite, may not have had a sales background. She offered to put something together for them, and the idea for the book was born.

Audri is a native of Cleveland, Ohio. She graduated from Cleveland State University with a major in International Marketing. Here is where she met and married her husband, Roderick, and raised her son, Langston. She has also called a few other wonderful cities home to include, Chicago, Atlanta, and Los Angeles. She continues to enjoy writing, traveling, cooking, and is currently working in recruiting

CPSIA information can be obtained
at www.ICGtesting.com
Printed in the USA
FSHW020525030222
88099FS

9 781649 529701